Let's Make

Trail Mix

by Mari Bolte

NORWOOD**H**OUSE**P**RESS

Norwood House Press

For information regarding Norwood House Press, please visit our website at:
www.norwoodhousepress.com or call 866-565-2900.

PHOTO CREDITS: page 4: ©Madisyn Reppucci / EyeEm / Getty Images; page 7: ©Ana-Maria Tegzes / Shutterstock; page 8: ©Monkey Business Images / Shutterstock; page 11: ©Rosa Herrara; page 12: ©zarzamora / Shutterstock; page 15: ©Krasula / Shutterstock; page 16: ©wavebreakmedia / Shutterstock; page 19: ©Rosa Herrara; page 21: ©Salena Stinchcombe / Shutterstock; page 22: ©Rosa Herrara; page 23: ©Rosa Herrara; page 24: ©Rosa Herrara; page 27: ©Rosa Herrara; page 28: ©Rosa Herrara

Hardcover ISBN: 978-1-68450-775-7
Paperback ISBN: 978-1-68404-756-7

LIBRARY OF CONGRESS CATALOGING-IN-PUBLICATION DATA
Library of Congress Cataloging-in-Publication Data has been filed and is available at catalog.loc.gov

353N—082022
Manufactured in the United States of America in North Mankato, Minnesota.

Contents

National Trail Mix Day is August 31. Many people celebrate by making their own snack blend.

CHAPTER 1

All about Trail Mix

Get ready to go on an adventure! Grab your shoes, a backpack, and a water bottle. You're going to need **energy** too. So don't forget a bag of trail mix!

The food we carry with us needs to get us through the challenges of the day. Not all to-go food is good for that, though. Trail mix is the perfect blend of dried fruits and nuts to help people stay active all day.

People have been eating on the go for thousands of years. **Indigenous** people on the Great Plains had a travel food called pemmican. It was made from dried meat, melted fat, and dried fruit.

Pemmican was easy to carry. It could be eaten right away or turned into a soup or stew. And it would last a long time. Some people say up to 50 years!

Immigrants to the American frontier learned how to make pemmican. They ate and traded it.

Finding a quick, easy-to-eat snack has always been a problem to solve. Danish students ate a snack called "student oats" in the 1800s. It had raisins and almonds. On special occasions, they'd add chocolate.

People on the Great Plains used buffalo meat and fat to make pemmican. In the Pacific Northwest, it was made with fish.

In 1906, outdoorsman Horace Kephart published *The Book of Camping and Woodcraft.* He suggested carrying a handful of nuts, raisins, and a bit of chocolate for energy on the trail. People started calling it "GORP." That stands for Good Old Raisins and Peanuts, or Granola, Oats, Raisins, and Peanuts, depending on who you ask.

When active, your body needs more fuel. Choosing a healthy snack is important!

Today, trail mix is sold in stores around the world. People in the United States spend more than $1.2 billion on snack and nut mixes every year.

People enjoy trail mix while outdoors. They also keep it in gym bags or backpacks for between-meal snacking. Trail mix can be added to salads as toppers, mixed into yogurt, or put on top of ice cream.

Peanuts are the most popular nuts in the world. Most of them are used for peanut butter. But other nuts have been replacing peanuts in trail mix. Peanut **allergies** have become more common. In the United States, the number of kids with peanut allergies has tripled over the past 20 years. Walnuts and pistachios are becoming more popular alternatives.

People are also more concerned about the foods they eat. Alternative diets often include more nuts. Paleo, gluten-free, and plant-based diets all rely on the foods found in trail mix. People who eat paleo try to stick to foods found by hunting or gathering. Gluten-free diets do not include wheat products. And plant-based diets focus on fruits, vegetables, nuts, seeds, and other foods from plant sources.

When you think of trail mix, you probably think "healthy snack." The basic recipe of fruit, nuts, and chocolate hasn't changed. But trail mix can be customized to add the things you like best.

Some trail mix combines sweet and salty. Sweet chocolate chips or candies are classic. Butterscotch or white or dark chocolate chips are just as delicious. Chocolate-covered fruit, nuts, and seeds are two ingredients in one! Nuts can come salted or unsalted. Other salty choices are potato chips and popcorn. Salt helps our body keep a healthy blood pressure. It also encourages us to drink more water.

You can add flavors from around the world to your trail mix. Try Asian flavors like wasabi peas or rice crackers. Wasabi peas are roasted peas. They are seasoned with a spicy flavoring called wasabi. Fried lentils or chickpeas are other things to try. Chia seeds and quinoa are healthy additions that originated in South America.

Parts of Trail Mix

A handful of dried fruit doesn't weigh much, but it's full of the things the body needs.

CHAPTER 2

Make Your Own Trail Mix

Trail mix is a "complete food." This means it has **carbohydrates**, proteins, and fats. Carbohydrates are your body's main source of energy. **Fiber** and sugars are carbohydrates. So are **starches**.

Dried fruit has lots of fibers and sugars. They are absorbed quickly. They give the body bursts of energy.

Fruit is made up of a lot of water. When it is dried, it shrinks. The nutrients, sugars, and calories become **concentrated**.

Nuts and seeds have protein, which helps you feel alert. Protein helps your body feel full faster. It also helps your bones and muscles grow and get strong.

Seeds and nuts are similar. Both are full of protein, vitamins, minerals, and fiber. It takes the body longer to digest fiber. The **glucose** and nutrients in nuts and seeds are released slowly into the body. That's how you get the energy to stay active all day.

Seeds and nuts are also full of healthy fats. When the body uses up the energy from the proteins and carbohydrates, the fat in trail mix gets used next.

Peanuts have the highest level of protein out of any nut. One ounce of peanuts has 7.3 grams of protein.

16

Chocolate adds a sweet flavor and goes well with dried fruit. It also has fats. Dark chocolate is full of antioxidants. These are substances found in fruits and vegetables, including cocoa. Antioxidants can have health benefits. They can help prevent diseases like **diabetes**.

Dark chocolate is also full of iron. Iron is good for increased blood flow. The better your blood flows, the more oxygen your body gets during exercise.

Not everyone can have chocolate. **Carob** is a good replacement. Unlike chocolate, carob does not have **caffeine**. White chocolate is another option. Although it is made from cocoa beans, it's different from regular chocolate. Or try yogurt chips!

Drinking water with trail mix helps the nutrients break down and get absorbed by the body.

Homemade trail mix should be mixed just before eating. Even when stored in an airtight container, it is at its best for only a couple of days. When two different ingredients are mixed together, moisture is exchanged. This is called moisture **migration**.

You might think dried fruit doesn't have water. But it has some! That water moves around. How much it moves is called water **activity**. The moisture in food with a lot of water activity moves to food with less water activity. The water in a dried cranberry moves to a cashew, making the cashew soft and soggy. The cranberry is left dry and hard. This process can take just a few days. Moisture can cause other issues too. The sugar in dried fruit is more likely to grow and cause mold. The moisture can also cause nuts to go **rancid**. Store-bought trail mix is treated to keep all this from happening.

Materials Checklist

✓ 1 1/2 cups nuts and/or seeds

✓ 1/2 cup dried fruit

✓ 1/2 cup chocolate

✓ 1/2 cup mix-ins

✓ measuring cups

✓ large bowl

✓ spoon for stirring

✓ baggies or jars for storage

Mixing smaller amounts of trail mix at a time can help with portion control.

CHAPTER 3

In the Kitchen!

Now that you know what goes into trail mix, it's time to make your own! This recipe will make 3 cups of trail mix. A small amount of trail mix goes a long way. One serving of trail mix is just 1/4 cup. This recipe will make 12 servings.

1. Choose your nuts and seeds. Some options are peanuts, pecans, and walnuts. Try out pistachios or sunflower seeds. Almonds, cashews, pumpkin seeds, or chia seeds are other choices.

The fat found in nuts and seeds is good for your heart and brain!

2. Add 1 1/2 cups of nuts and seeds to a large bowl.

3. Choose your dried fruit. Raisins, cranberries, and banana chips are classics. Apples, cherries, or pineapple are fun to try. Pineapple, coconut, or mangoes add a tropical twist.

4. Add 1/2 cup of dried fruit to the bowl.

5. Choose your chocolate. Chips and chunks are easy picks. Carob chips and cacao nibs might be nice to try. White or dark chocolate add new flavors and colors.

6. Add 1/2 cup of chocolate pieces to the bowl.

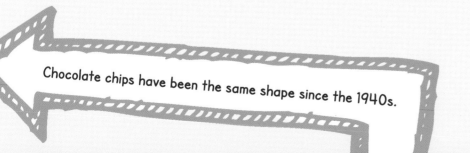

Chocolate chips have been the same shape since the 1940s.

7. Add 1/2 cup of mix-ins. Some fun options are granola, cereal, oats, wasabi peas, or jerky. Rice crackers, cheese curls, and bagel chips are others. Try yogurt clusters, graham crackers, or mini marshmallows. What about cheese crackers or popcorn?

8. Stir all your chosen ingredients together.

9. To keep track of portions, divide the mixture into quarter-cup servings. Divide them into baggies or jars. Eat within one or two days.

Once your trail mix is gone, make another batch. Add a different mix-in or two. The possibilities are endless!

Mix It Up!

Congratulations! You have made trail mix. Now see if there are ways to make it better. Use any of these changes and see how they improve your trail mix.

- Add seasoning for more flavor! Sprinkle BBQ dry rub, nutritional yeast, ranch powder, or your other favorite dry seasoning over your nuts and seeds. Spread out on a baking sheet. With an adult's help, bake at 325 degrees Fahrenheit for 10 minutes. Stir. Next, bake for another 10 minutes. Let cool completely. Then, add the rest of your trail mix ingredients.

- Make energy bombs by mixing 1 3/4 cup of your homemade trail mix with 1 cup quick oats, 1/2 cup peanut butter, and 1/4 cup maple syrup or honey. Roll into balls about 2 tablespoons in size. Store in the refrigerator for up to three weeks.

Glossary

activity (ak-TIV-uh-tee): movement

allergies (AL-ur-geez): a condition where the body reacts badly to certain foods or substances

caffeine (kaf-EEN): a chemical found in plants; caffeine stimulates the body's central nervous system

carbohydrates (kar-boh-HY-drayts): sugar molecules; along with protein and fat, carbohydrates are one of three main nutrients in foods and drinks

carob (kair-UHB): the fruit from a carob tree; when processed, carob is a sweet and healthy alternative to chocolate

concentrated (KAHN-suhn-tray-ted): stronger or more flavorful after removing water

diabetes (die-uh-BEE-teez): a disease that keeps the body from producing or reacting to the hormone insulin

energy (EN-ur-gee): the strength to do something

fiber (FY-buhr): the parts of a plant your body can't digest or absorb

glucose (GLOO-kose): a natural sugar found in plants and their fruit

immigrants (IM-uh-gruhnts): people who move to a foreign country

Indigenous (in-DIH-juh-nuss): native to a particular place

migration (my-GRAY-shuhn): movement from one place to another

rancid (RAN-sid): smelling or tasting bad due to being old or stale

starches (STAR-chez): powdery white substances found in plants and foods such as rice and potatoes

For More Information

Books

Bellisario, Gina. *Eat for Energy: Choose Good Foods.* Minneapolis, MN: Lerner Publications, 2022.

Hughes, Sloane. *My Stomach.* Minneapolis, MN: Bearport Publishing Company, 2022.

Thomas, Rachael L. *Create a Camp Kitchen Your Way!: Making Cooking and Eating Tools.* Minneapolis, MN: Super Sandcastle, an imprint of ABDO Publishing, 2020.

Websites

A Kids Guide to Exploring the Great Outdoors (https://www.aaastateofplay.com/a-kids-guide-to-exploring-the-great-outdoors/) Find out what you need to get outdoors, and then do it!

KidsHealth (https://kidshealth.org/en/kids/digestive-system.html) Learn about your digestive system.

MyPlate (https://www.myplate.gov/life-stages/kids) Learn about nutrition from the US Department of Agriculture.

Index

About the Author

Mari Bolte has worked in publishing as a writer and editor for more than 15 years. She has written dozens of books about things like science and craft projects, historical figures and events, and pop culture. She lives in Minnesota.